ISBN-13: 9798373214209

Cover design by: North Star

BELIEVE

"We Believe In You."
Swanky & Lamp

Swanky Genius The Bird   **Lamp The Cat**

www.swankygenius.com

**Swanky Genius The Bird & Lamp The Cat
are whimsical pals who share uplifting messages for all!**

ABOUT THE AUTHOR

With a diverse background in business, the arts and
psychology, Peshah has helped many through
counseling, coaching, mentoring and building
businesses. Formally educated in Art Therapy, Instructional
Technology and Electronic Commerce, well traveled
throughout the USA, with time spent in Europe and Mexico,
Peshah's passion is to continue to inspire others
to live the life they truly desire.

Peshah is the owner and creator of the 1213 Jewelry line.

ABOUT THE ILLUSTRATOR

North Star's ilustrative illuminations bring to life the
Swanky Genius series."Lamp The Cat" and "Swanky
Genius The Bird" are whimsical best pals who express the
heartfelt message of uplifting artists and creators.

North star is a vibrant, ingenius artist. Having always been a creative
soul, North Star is an ardent LEGO Builder, a skater, a keyboard and
guitar artist, an avid reader, loves to travel, and, of course, adores cats!

SWANKY GENIUS®

CAUSES THE AUTHOR SUPPORTS

Peshah, the Swanky Genius author, is
the creator of 1213 Jewelry

Community Projects
Organizations & Causes
supported by
1213 Jewelry

Advocates For Freedom - ending human exploitation

V-Day - stopping violence against women and girls

Disability Connection - creating community for the disabled

Fatherless & Widows - help for widows and fatherless children

Global Maritime Ministries - assisting maritime workers

Back Bay Mission - raising people out of poverty

Token Of Love - ending cycles of abuse, poverty and addiction

and many more causes
www.1213jewelry.com.

10 WAYS TO NO LONGER BEING A DEPRESSED ARTIST

*"This book is dedicated to you being
a happy and prosperous artist."*
Swanky & Lamp

*Genius is Latin for guiding spirit;
the soul behind all art and innovation.
Each building, each maestro, has a genius.*

WHY A BIRD?

Why is my name "Swanky Genius the Bird"?

"Genius" had a different meaning in earlier times, than in present day.

The originial Latin definition was:
"A guiding spirit that gives birth to one's creativity".

One cannot be born without a genius. Everyone has this guide,
throughout their entire lives, helping them express their abilities.

Swanky Genius The Bird
is your personal genius -
overlooking, accompanying and guiding you
in the creative endeavors that are your life.

Birds have a long historical presence as messengers of love,
rebirth, nobility, wisdom, victory and hope.

So whom better than a little sweet bird to be your own personal genius,
accompanying you and your creations *on your beautiful life's path?*

CONTENTS

Copyright

Believe

About The Author

About The Illustrator

Causes The Author Supports

10 Ways To No Longer Being A Depressed Artist

Why a Bird?

Starving Artists 1

Who Artists Really Are 3

Your True Essence 5

You Don't Have To Market Your Art 7

Look Up 10

Tiny Changes 12

Deeds Of Loveliness 14

Visual Identity 16

Be Kind To You 19

Lost Confidence 21

Thank You 23

Your Heart 25

My Social Media 27

Swanky Genius Book Series 29

Miracles 31

STARVING ARTISTS

"Yes, yes, of course you can."
Swanky Genius

The term "starving artist" deters so many of us from following our dreams of creativity and contribution.

So the first favor I am going to ask of you, please, is:

"Would you be willing to no longer use the words 'starving artist' to describe yourself?".

I know some of us do it to be funny or to relate to our artist friends but, deep down inside, we feel sad every time we utter those words. Because we know that we were put on this earth to share our art, to help lift the hearts of humanity and to shed light on a struggling world.

So please, kindred spirit, let's find beautiful new words to describe ourselves.

Try saying these sentences out loud and tell me how they make you feel?

"I love creating."

"I am on this planet to spread happiness through my art."

"I am honored to have been imbued with deep creative abilities."

"My legacy is to leave an artistic imprint on this planet that noone else can."

Would you be willing to speak one of these statements out loud every day, for the next seven days?

You can put a little check mark next to each day on your calendar after you declare one of these statements.

"Please let me help you to
remember who you truly are
and why you are here."
Swanky Genius

WHO ARTISTS REALLY ARE

"You are waking up from the dream.
You are a powerful creator.
Remember who you truly are."
Swanky Genius

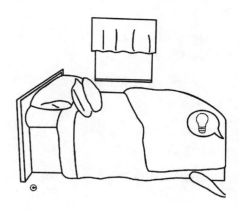

There was a time in history when artists were so highly valued. They were considered to be wise, insightful and great contributors to life. They held a certain place in their society that was quietly respected by all.

You are that person; you are.

Let us remember to revere who we are - the creators, the artists, the builders who take what is unseen and make it into the seen, for all to enjoy.

You may think your talents are not important, that there are others who are more gifted, who have honed and refind their art forms more than you have.

That is not so.

What you have been imbued with - the gifts, talents, abilities and their modes of expression -

no one else can do what you can do.

No one.

Today, you can take one step in the direction of your art form.

You can write several lines for your next song and hang it on your refrigerator.

You can paint a few strokes, screenshot it and make it your phone's lock screen image.

You can take photographs of the beautiful day, print out your favorite one and hang it by your bed.

You can write the opening lines for your play, with lipstick, on your bathroom mirror.

You can name the characters for your novel, write them on little notes and tuck one inside each coffee cup.

You can play and record the couple of cords you know you want in your next song, then set this recording as the ringtone for whenever a text comes through.

"Please let me help you to
place reminders of your talents
sprinkled throughout your daily life."
Swanky Genius

YOUR TRUE ESSENCE

"You already are that which you desire to be."
Swanky Genius

It is interesting how we project who we want to be, into the future.

We think it is someday, years from now, when something definitive happens - then we will be who we were created to be.

We think that when we receive a specific opportunity, when a breakthrough occurs for our art, that then we will be a success, then we will be who we were created to be.

You already are that which you desire to be. You already are beautiful, gifted, talented, insightful, amazing.

You've just forgotten that is your true essence.

It is time to remember who you already are.

Seasons change.

In this season you can change how you see yourself; you can see your true essence.

How?

Catch yourself.

Catch yourself every time you are about to utter something other than loving or kind about you.

Just stop. Consider. Be willing to not say that.

Little by little, moment by moment - every time you make a choice not to say something unkind about yourself - the old image of you will fade away.

And naturally, in its place, life will fill in those empty spaces you've created. Life will filter in others who say gentle words toward you, others who reflect back to you the true beauty of who you are.

> *"Please let me help you to*
> *make space for kindness*
> *to enter into your sacred life."*
> *Swanky Genius*

YOU DON'T HAVE TO MARKET YOUR ART

"So let's marry
your art to your heart
and connect you
to your world again."
Swanky Genius

I have a second favor to ask, please.

"Would you be willing to stop using terminology such as 'marketing my art'?"

Somehow, recently "marketing" snuck in alongside the word "art" and terrified and alienated many artists.

How many artists love to create but have no interest in "marketing" their art? You want people to appreciate your work and purchase it, without having to create an entire sales campaign.

You can.

You can sell alot of your art without feeling like you are selling.

How?

Align yourself with causes.

Ask yourself out loud, "Who do I want to help?".

Do you love to rescue animals? Are you dedicated to the earth being taken care of? Does it make your heart sing when you spend time with the elderly or with little children? Is there a favorite museum in your region that makes you happy every time you visit? Are there local gardens that bring you joy each time you stroll through them? Is there a part of your neighborhood that needs to be tended to?

You are an artist and you feel life deeply.

So let's marry your art to your heart and connect you to your world once again.

What should you do?

Create a "Community Project".

What is a Community Project?

A Community Project is an organic movement of artists affiliating themsleves with and contributing percentages of their art sales to causes and organizations.

How do you create your own Community Project?

Think of who you want to most help. What most pulls on your heart? What organization or cause would you love to contribute to, to support?

Then call them or stop by their local office.

Simply say this to the sweet person who works for the organization -

"I am an artist and I want to help your cause, through my art. I would like to:

create a painting,

write a song,

take photos,

sculpt,

design jewelry...

that represents your organization. And I am offering to contribute a percentage of the sales proceeds of this art to your cause. I am willing to set up at your fund raisers and events and tell people why I believe in the community work you do. I would consider it an honor to help support your cause."

Start with your heart. Align with your community.

"Please let me help you to
reconnect to your
heart and beliefs,
through your art."
Swanky Genius

LOOK UP

We creators worry alot.

Why does that happen so often?

Because we aren't looking up.

It is interesting; lightly track yourself throughout your day. Whenever you feel a heaviness, a worry, a concern arising, pause for a moment.

You will notice something fascinating.

You are looking down. You are physically looking downward, not upward.

And something else that is fascinating - if you raise your eyes up, you cannot stay in that down feeling.

Because when our eyes are downward, we are very introspective, very caught in the myriad of thoughts and considerations about what may happen in life.

But when we raise our eyes upward, when we look up, our perspective shifts.

You can feel it.

And when we are looking up, possibilities and an openness to life comes into our view.

To help you to "look up" more -

You can design a "wall of suggestions", a place in your dwelling and dedicate it to what inspires your heart; a place to "look up" to.

You can fill that space with notes, sayings, quotes that cause you to think, to consider, in a way you may not be accustomed to.

The more often you look up, the more often you read from your "wall of suggestions", the lighter your heart will feel.

And you deserve to be lighthearted.

> *"Let me help you to*
> *remember to look up,*
> *because upward is the direction*
> *you are headed in."*
> *Swanky Genius*

TINY CHANGES

"You winning is inevitable."
Swanky Genius

Expansion.

It is inevitable. Your winning is inevitable.

It is the nature of life and all that is.

Your art will evolve and expand; you will also because you and your art are one. There is no separation between you and what you create.

How can that be?

Because without you, your art form could not appear in this world. And without your art, you would not be you.

What can you do so that the sharing of your art with many more occurs? How can that be guaranteed?

By immersing yourself more in life.

Since you and your art are inseparable, when you immerse yourself more in life, your creativity will naturally expand also. And then, then opportunities appear on your path.

So what does immersing yourself more in life look like?

It may be taking a walk in the rain. It may be driving home from the grocery store via a different route. It may be getting your favorite cup of tea from a cafe other than the one closest to your home.

And what happens when you make just those tiny changes?

Life happens.

Unusual encounters happens.

You meet someone you would not have met otherwise, at your usual tea cafe.

You are inspired by something you see during that walk in the rain.

On your different route from the grocery store you notice a record shop you didn't realize was in your town, and you find your favorite album from when you were fifteen.

And then what happens?

You expand a little and your art expands a little and then the trajectory of your life expands a little.

One seemingly tiny change, linked to another and another seemingly tiny change, and then, then expansion appears one day, without any introduction, and now, now new opportunities have appeared on your life's horizon.

Welcome to the expanded version of you and your art.

"Let me help you to
be courageous enough
to make tiny changes,
that will bring
expansive opportunities."
Swanky Genius

DEEDS OF LOVELINESS

"It will arrive in an unexpected way."
Swanky Genius

May I ask a third favor of you, please?

"Would you be willing to encourage one artist every week?".

When you lift their spirit, you will lift your own too.

We have a tendency to think that other creators are so confident, that all is going well for them, that they never feel insecure about their art.

But, in actuality, other artists are just like you and me.

They feel lonely or isolated, they feel like they do not fit in, in this world.

They think they are too sensitive, too introspective.

Other creators lose focus and drive, just as we do.

So once a week, find an artist you can uplift.

You can comment on their social media posts, letting them know you find their art form to be beautiful.

You can stop by their studio on a rainy day when they are sad that not many shoppers have come by.

You can talk to them at a market where they are set up and allow them to share their heart with you. You can listen as they tell stories about the challenges they've met with lately.

You can bring a little gift to them, at their shop.

You can make sandwiches or bake cookies and drop them off at a show or their studio.

You can ship a piece of your art to them, with a hand written note card, letting them know you value what they contribute to the world.

There are truly endless ways to encourage a kindred spirit.

I am sure you will discover your own acts of kindness that can touch another creator's heart.

And your deed of loveliness will lift your soul too.

You will realize you are not alone.

You will know that another artist feels life as you do.

> *"Please allow me to help you to*
> *reconnect to other artists,*
> *because we really are all one."*
> *Swanky Genius*

VISUAL IDENTITY

"Tell a different story."
Swanky Genius

You are your brand.

What does that mean?

You have a message you want to share with the world.

You have a vision of what you want your art to bring to others lives.

You have a purpose in your heart that is the reason behind your creations.

That is your brand.

You are your brand.

And when you develop a name for your art and a "logo" and "mission statement", you now have a vehicle with which to easily share the purpose behind your art.

And, you are recognizable.

Because whenever an individual or gallery or organization sees your logo, they know it is you.

Your art is connected to your brand, your personhood is connected to your brand, and now, now you and your art are easily recognizable.

This is your "Visual Identity".

Somehow the idea of an artist having a logo and a mission statement became relegated as "too much like a business", too corporate, too uncreative.

But having an identifiable way for others to recognize your unique persona is anything but "corporate".

Think back in time, about artists you admire, those whose lives are shared within the history books. Did not each artist have certain ways, beliefs and styles of communication that they were known for?

If we separate the terms "logo" and "mission statement" from what we consider the sedate and confined business realm - well, the idea of being recognizable as an artist is actually a great benefit.

How much easier is it to tell someone what you prefer as a gift if you know the "name brand" of that item? How much simpler is it to explain the car you like to drive if you know the model name? How much breezier is it for your friend to pick up your favorite snack from the grocery store if they know what company makes the snack?

You and your art deserve to be that recognizable.

So how do you create a logo and a mission statement to represent you and your art?

And once you've designed it, what purpose does it serve?

Consider the reason behind why you create.

Is it to bring love to the world? Does your art purpose to raise consciousness? Is your creative modality generational and you want that skill to be passed on?

Sketch out that meaning in a notebook. What colors and shapes express the purpose behind your art? What words define why you create.

And just as you introduce yourself by your name, your art now has an identity of her own. Her logo, her mission statement.

And now, now you can easily share her with the world. And she will gain the recognition she deserves, because now, now she is easily identifiable.

Your art deserves that.

"Please allow me to help you to
give your art a defineable identity."
Swanky Genius

BE KIND TO YOU

"Honor yourself."
Swanky Genius

The little things matter.

There are so many ways to be kind to yourself, and that really does matter.

The tendency for artists to be too hard on themselves is, well, more than a tendency.

It is a pattern many of us have gotten into, a groove where if we feel we haven't accomplished the level of success we believe we should have thus far - well, we are just unkind to ourselves.

We pigeon-hole ourselves as somehow less deserving.

We say that when we have our work in a certain gallery, when we receive a specific amount of orders - then we will feel good, then we will take better care of ourselves.

You are not separate from your art.

You are one with your creations.

So if you aren't being kind to you, you are not being kind to your artistic expression either.

What can you do to soften your world a little bit, to be gentler with you, as the creator of the creations?

You can keep incense or candles in your abode so when you use them the atmosphere in your home is more peaceful. You can buy yourself a book every month, one that will lift your spirit. You can play one of your favorite songs, leaving it on repeat, until your heart feels full once again. You can create little notes with one inspirational word on each, and scatter them throughout your drawers and cabinets.

You deserve kindness.

And when you are kind to yourself, your art, which is you, will be happier too.

"Please allow me to
help you honor yourself."
Swanky Genius

LOST CONFIDENCE

"Follow your heart.
You have the innate power to
make your dreams come true."
Swanky Genius

Fear is something we will encounter.

It is part of the fabric of life, particularly for creators.

Why?

Because we usually are living outside of the conformities of society, even if only by the way we choose to support ourselves financially.

But remember what I shared with you at the beginning of our journey?

Artists used to be considered very highly.

And they can, and will be, again.

It is just that we creators have lost our confidence.

We came to believe that what we have to offer life doesn't really matter after all.

But that is not so.

Art is an integral aspect of every day life. It is so sublimely incorporated into what we do and how we live.

The music we listen to as we are driving, the song we sing to our plants or our children, the way we bake our cookies that is just a little bit different than what the recipe calls for. Even the way we fold our laundry or write our grocery shopping lists.

Creativity is everywhere. All of the time.

But we artists have come to believe a story that sounds like this -

"Your art cannot support you."

"You need to have a day job and explore your art only as a hobby."

"Unless you are accepted by a major museum or gallery, you will never succeed."

And many more stories like these, we tell ourselves over and over, until we believe them.

Then fear arises.

But, these are just stories.

And we have the innate ability to create new stories.

And when we create new stories, the fear will leave.

Because we will see momentum build as artists are following their heart's desire, uplifting one another, supporting community causes and ultimately sharing their gifts, talents and abilities with the world.

"Please allow me to help you to
know that the gifts you have
within yourself, the world needs."
Swanky Genius

THANK YOU

*"Thank you for allowing us to
help you remember who you are."*
Swanky & Lamp

Swanky Genius The Bird   **Lamp The Cat**

www.swankygenius.com

YOUR HEART

"Start with your heart.
Align with your community."
Swanky Genius

Peshah has mentored artists
and creators since 2003.

Her expertise has helped artists to evolve their skills
into viable businesses
by building a brand
and displaying confidence
in their creative expressions.

The creators she has advised and counseled
span a diverse sector of art genres including
soap makers, photographers, tie dye artists,
glass molders, sculptors, pepper jelly makers
and t-shirt designers.

Peshah's desire is to see artists succeed financially
and feel uplifted in their creative careers.

MY SOCIAL MEDIA

@1213.jewelry
@swankygenius
@reallampthecat

1213jewelry.com
swankygenius.com

For bulk book/journal orders,
speaking engagements and podcast appearances,
please contact Peshah at
hello@swankygenius.com

SWANKY GENIUS BOOK SERIES

"10 WAYS TO NO LONGER BEING A DEPRESSED ARTIST"

Is part of the
COMMUNITY PROJECTS
Series

Other books, journals & coloring books in the
Community Projects series include:

"21 Ways To Make The World Beautiful" Journal

"21 Ways Artists Save The World" Journal

"Swanky & Lamp's World" Coloring Book

www.swankygenius.com

MIRACLES

I thank God for all of the blessings
life has brought. Although my journey
has been filled with many challenges,
the hope which God planted
within me has
helped me
to forge forward.

*I always believe for miracles,
for all of God's children and creations.*

*Much peace always,
Peshah*

Made in the USA
Columbia, SC
18 June 2024

36821425R00026